D0999183

PROJECTIVE ORNAMENT

by

Claude Bragdon

DOVER PUBLICATIONS, INC.

NEW YORK

Published in Canada by General Publishing Company, Ltd.,
30 Lesmill Road, Don Mills, Toronto, Ontario.

Published in the United Kingdom by Constable and Company,
Ltd., 3 The Lanchesters, 162–164 Fulham Palace Road, London
W6 9ER.

This Dover edition, first published in 1992, is an unabridged
republication of the work originally published by The Manas
Press, Rochester, New York, in 1915. The original frontispiece
(by Frederick L. Trautmann) has been moved to the front cover of
this edition. A reproduction of Albrecht Dürer's *Melencolia I* (see
Chapter VI) has been added as the frontispiece to this edition.

Manufactured in the United States of America
Dover Publications, Inc., 31 East 2nd Street, Mineola, N.Y.
11501

Library of Congress Cataloging-in-Publication Data

Bragdon, Claude Fayette, 1866–1946
    Projective ornament / Claude Bragdon.
        p.   cm.
    Reprint. Originally published: Rochester, N.Y. : Manas
Press, 1915.
    ISBN 0-486-27117-X
    1. Decoration and ornament.   2. Fourth dimension.   I.
Title.
NK1570.B7   1992
745.4—dc20   91–46978
                                                                CIP

DEDICATED TO E. B.

CONTENTS

FOREWORD

MANY sincere workers in the field of art have realized the aesthetic poverty into which the modern world has fallen. Designers are reduced either to dig in the boneyard of dead civilizations, or to develop a purely personal style and method. The latter is rarely successful: city dwellers that we are for the most part, and self-divorced from Nature, she witholds her intimate secrets from us. Our ignorance and superficiality stand pitifully revealed.

Is there not some source, some secret spring of fresh beauty undiscovered, to satisfy our thirsty souls? Having all his life asked himself this question, the author at last undertook its quest. Such results as have up to the present rewarded his search are here set forth. Their value and importance will be determined, as all things are determined, by use and time, but this much must be admitted—they are drawn from a deep well.

The author desires to acknowledge his indebtedness to the following sources for material contained in this volume: *The Fourth Dimension*, by C. Howard Hinton, M. A.; *Geometry of Four Dimensions*, by Henry Parker Manning, Ph. D.; *Observational Geometry*, by William T. Campbell, A. M.; *Mathematical Essays and Recreations*, by Hermann

Schubert; also to an essay entitled *Regular Figures in n-dimensional Space*, by W. I. Stringham, in the third volume of the American Journal of Mathematics, and an article on *Magic Squares* in the Eleventh Edition of the Encyclopaedia Britannica.

The chapter entitled *A Philosophy of Ornament* is enriched by certain ideas first suggested in a lecture by Mr. Irving K. Pond. With no desire to wear borrowed plumes, the author yet found it impossible in this instance to avoid doing so, they are so woven into the very texture of his thought. In the circumstances he can only make grateful acknowledgement to Mr. Pond.

The author desires to express his gratitude to Mr. Frederick L. Trautmann for his admirable interpretations of Projective Ornament in color, of which the front cover gives an idea—and only an idea.

I

THE NEED OF A NEW FORM LANGUAGE

We are without a form language suitable to the needs of today. Architecture and ornament constitute such a language. Structural necessity
may be depended upon to evolve fit and expressive architectural forms,
but the same thing is not true of ornament. This necessary element
might be supplied by an individual genius, it might be derived from
the conventionalization of natural forms, or lastly it might be developed from geometry. The geometric source is richest in promise.

ARCHITECTURE AND ORNAMENT

IN contemplating the surviving relics of any period
in which the soul of a people achieved aesthetic
utterance through the arts of space, it is clear that
in their architecture and in their ornament they had
a form language as distinctive and adequate as any
spoken language. Today we have no such language.
This is equivalent to saying that we have not at-
tained to aesthetic utterance through the arts of
space. That we shall attain to it, that we shall
develop a new form language, it is impossible to
doubt; but not until after we realize our need, and
set about supplying it.

Consider the present status of architecture, which is preëminently the art of space. Modern

Pentahedroids

architecture, except on its engineering side, has not yet found itself: the style of a building is determined, not by necessity, but by the whim of the designer; it is made up of borrowings and survivals. So urgent is the need of more appropriate and indigenous architectural forms with which to clothe the steel framework for which some sort of protective covering is of first importance, that some architects have ceased searching in the cemetery of a too sacredly cherished past. They are seeking to solve their problems rather by a process of elimination, using the most elementary forms and the materials readiest to hand. In thus facing their difficulty they are re-creating their chosen art, and not abrogating it.

The development of new architectural forms appropriate to the new structural methods is already under way, and its successful issue may safely be left to necessity and to time; but the no less urgent need of fresh motifs in ornament has not yet even begun to be met. So far as architecture is concerned, the need is acute only for those who are determined to be modern. Having perforce abandoned the structural methods of the past, and the forms associated with these methods, they nevertheless continue to use the ornament associated with what they have abandoned: the clothes are new, but not the collar and necktie. The reason for this failure of invention is that while common sense, and a feeling for fitness and proportion, serve to produce the clothing of a building, the faculty for originating appropriate and beautiful ornament is one of the rarest in the whole range of art. Those arts of space which involve the element of decoration suffer from the same lack, and for a similar reason.

Three possible sources of supply suggest themselves for this needed element in a new form language. Ornament might be the single-handed creation of an original genius in this partic-ular field; it might be de-rived from the conventional-ization of native flora, as it was in the past; or it might be developed from geometry. Let us examine each of these possibilities in turn.

The first we must reject. Even supposing that this art saviour should appear as some rarely gifted and resourceful creator of ornament, it would be calamitous to impose the idiosyncratic space rhythm of a single individual upon an entire architecture. Fortu-

Tesseracts: Cubes

nately such a thing is impossible. In Mr. Louis Sullivan, for example, we have an ornamentalist

3

of the highest distinction (quite aside from his sterling qualities as an architect), but from the work of his imitators it is clear that his secret is incommunicable. It would be better for his disciples to develop an individual manner of their own, and this a few of them are doing. Mr. Sullivan will leave his little legacy of beauty for the enrichment of those who come after, but our hope for an ornament less personal, more universal and generic, will be as far from realization as before.

Tetrahedrons: Tesseracts: Icositetrahedroid

NATURE

Such a saviour being by the very necessities of the case denied us, may we not go directly to Nature and choose whatever patterns suit our fancy from the rich garment which she weaves and wears? There is no lack of precedent for such a procedure. The Egyptian lotus, the Greek honeysuckle, the acanthus, the Indian palmette, achieved, in this way, their apotheosis in art. The Japanese use their chrysanthemum, their wisteria and bamboo, in similar fashion; so why may not we do likewise? The thing has already been attempted, but never consistently nor successfully.

While far from solving the problem of a new language of ornament, for reasons presently to appear, the conventionalization of our native grains, fruits and flowers, would undoubtedly introduce a note of fresh beauty and appropriateness into our architecture. Teachers of design might put the problem of such conventionalizations before their pupils to their advantage, and to the advancement of art. There is, however, one difficulty that presents itself. By reason of scientific agriculture, intensive cultivation under glass, and because of the ease and freedom of present-day transportation, vegetation in civilized countries has lost much of its local character and significance. Corn, buck-

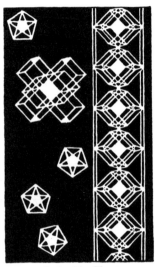

Pentahedroids: Tesseracts

wheat, cotton, tobacco, though native to America, are less distinctively American than they once were. Moreover, dwellers in cities, where for the most part the giant flora of architecture lifts its skyscraping heads, know nothing of buckwheat except in pancakes, of cotton except as cloth or in the bale. Corn in the can is more familiar to them than corn on the cob, and not one smoker in ten would recognize tobacco as it grows in the fields. Our divorce from nature has become so complete that we no longer dwell in the old-time intimate communion with her visible forms.

GEOMETRY

There remains at least one other possibility, and it is that upon which we shall now concentrate all our attention, for it seems indeed an open door. Geometry and number are at the root of every kind of formal beauty. That the tapestry of nature is woven on a mathematical framework is known to every sincere student. As Emerson says, "Nature geometrizes . . . moon, plant, gas, crystal, are concrete geometry and number." Art is nature selected, arranged, sublimated, triply refined, but still nature, however refracted in and by consciousness. If art is a higher power of nature, the former must needs submit itself to mathematical analysis too. The larger aspect of this whole matter—the various vistas that the application of geometry to design opens up—has been treated by the author in a previous volume*. Narrowed down to the subject of ornament, our question is, what promise does geometry hold of a new ornamental mode?

Tesseract

In the past, geometry has given birth to many characteristic and consistent systems of ornamentation, and from its very nature is capable of giving

*The Beautiful Necessity.

6

birth to many more. Much of Hindu, Chinese, and Japanese ornament was derived from geometry, yet these all differ from one another, and from Moorish ornament, which owes its origin to the same source. Gothic tracery, from Perpendicular to Flamboyant, is nothing but a system of straight lines, circles, and the intersecting arcs of circles, variously arranged and combined. The interesting development of ornament in Germany which has taken place of late years, contains few elements other than the square and the circle, the parallelogram and the ellipse. It is a remarkable fact that ornamentation, in its primitive manifestations, is geometrical rather than naturalistic, though the geometrical source is the more abstract and purely intellectual of the two. Is not this a point in its favor? The great war undoubtedly ends an era: "the old order changeth." Our task is to create the art of the future: let us then draw our inspiration from the deepest, purest well.

Geometry is an inexhaustible well of formal beauty from which to fill our bucket; but before the draught is fit for use it should be examined, analyzed, and filtered through the consciousness of the artist.

If with the zeal of the convert we set at once to work with T square and compass to devise a new system of ornament from geometry, we shall probably end where we began. Let us, therefore, by a purely intellectual process of analysis and selection, try to discover some system of geometrical forms and configurations which shall yield that new ornamental mode of which we are in search.

II

ORNAMENT AND PSYCHOLOGY

Ornament is the outgrowth of no practical necessity, but of a striving toward beauty. Our zeal for efficiency has resulted in a corresponding aesthetic infertility. Signs are not lacking that consciousness is now looking in a new direction—away from the contemplation of the facts of materiality towards the mysteries of the supersensuous life. This transfer of attention should give birth to a new aesthetic, expressive of the changing psychological mood. The new direction of consciousness is well suggested in the phrase, *The Fourth Dimension of Space*, and the decorative motifs of the new aesthetic may appropriately be sought in four-dimensional geometry.

THE ORNAMENTAL MODE AND THE PSYCHOLOGICAL MOOD

ARCHITECTURAL forms and features, such as the column, the lintel, the arch, the vault, are the outgrowth of structural necessity, but this is not true of ornament. Ornament develops not from the need and the power to build, but from the need and the power to beautify. Arising from a psychological impulse rather than from a physical necessity, it reflects the national and racial consciousness. To such a degree is this true that any mutilated and time-worn fragment out of the great past when art was a language can without difficulty be assigned its place and period. Granted a dependence of the ornamental mode upon the psychological mood, our first business is to discover what that mood may be.

A great change has come over the collective consciousness: we are turning from the accumulation of facts to the contemplation of mysteries. Science is discovering infirmities in the very foundations of knowledge. Mathematics, through the questioning of certain postulates accepted as axiomatic for thousands of years, is concerning itself with problems not alone of one-, two-, and three-, but of *n*-dimensional spaces. Psychology, no longer content with superficial manifestations, is plunging deeper and deeper into the examination of the subconscious mind. Philosophy, despairing of translating life by the rational method, in terms of inertia, is attempting to apprehend the universal flux by the aid of intuition.

Icositetrahedroid

Religion is abandoning its man-made moralities of a superior prudence in favor of a quest for that mystical experience which foregoes all to gain all. In brief, there is a renascence of *wonder;* and art must attune itself to this new key-note of the modern world.

THE FOURTH DIMENSION

To express our sense of all this Newness many phrases have been invented. Of these *the Fourth Dimension* has obtained a currency quite outside the domain of mathematics, where it originated, and is frequently used as a synonym for what is new and

10

strange. But a sure intuition lies behind this loose use of a loose phrase—the perception, namely, that consciousness is moving in a new direction; that it is glimpsing vistas which it must needs explore.

Here, then, is the hint we have been seeking: consciousness is moving towards the conquest of a new space; ornament must indicate this movement of consciousness; geometry is the field in which we have staked out our particular claim. It follows, therefore, that in the soil of the geometry of four dimensions we should plant our metaphysical spade.

The fourth dimension may be roughly defined as a direction at right angles to every known direction. It is a hyperspace related to our space of three dimensions as the surface of a solid is related to its volume; it is the withinness of the within, the outside of externality.

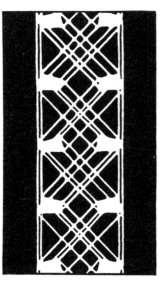

> "But this thou must not think to find
> With eyes of body but of mind."

We cannot point to it, we cannot picture it, though every point is the beginning of a pathway out of and into it.

Double Prisms

FOUR-DIMENSIONAL GEOMETRY

However little the mathematician may be prepared to grant the physical reality of hyperspace—or, more

11

properly, the hyperdimensionality of matter—its mathematical reality he would never call in question. Our plane and solid geometries are but the beginnings of this science. Four-dimensional geometry is far more extensive than three-dimensional. The number of figures, and their variety, increases more and more rapidly as we mount to higher and higher spaces, each space extending in a direction not existing in the next lower space. Moreover, these figures of hyperspace, though they are unknown to the senses, are known to the mind in great minuteness of detail.

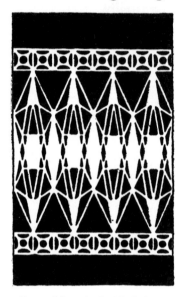

Base of Icosahedroid: Cubes

To the artist the richness of the field is not of great importance. He need concern himself with only a few of the more elementary figures of four-dimensional geometry, and only the most cursory acquaintance with the mathematical concepts involved in this geometry will give him all the material he seeks.

In the ensuing exposition, the willfulness and impatience of the artistic temperament towards everything it cannot turn to practical account will be indulged to the extent of omitting all explanations and speculations not strictly germane to the purely aesthetic aspect of the matter. To such readers as are disposed to dig deeper, however, the author's

A Primer of Higher Space may be found useful, and there is besides a literature upon the subject.

If after reviewing this literature the reader is disposed to regard the fourth dimension as a mere mathematical convention, it matters not in the least, so long as he is able to make practical use of it. He may likewise, with equal justice, question the existence of minus quantities, for example, but they produce practical results.

With this brief explanation the author now turns up his shovelful, leaving it to the discerning to determine whether it contains any gold.

III

THE KEY TO PROJECTIVE ORNAMENT

The idea of a fourth dimension is in conformity with reason, however foreign to experience. By means of projective geometry it is possible to represent a polyhedron (a three-dimensional figure) in the two dimensions of a plane. By an extension of the same method it is no less possible to represent a polyhedroid (a four-dimensional figure). Such representations in plane projection of solids and hypersolids constitute the raw material of Projective Ornament.

THE DEVELOPMENT OF THE EQUILATERAL TRIANGLE IN HIGHER SPACES

THE concept of a fourth dimension is so simple that almost anyone can understand it if only he will not limit his thought of that which is possible by his opinion of that which is practicable. It is not reason, but experience, that balks at the idea of four mutually perpendicular directions. Grant, therefore, if only for the sake of intellectual adventure, that there is a direction towards which we cannot point, at right angles to every one of the so-called three dimensions of space, and then see where we are able to come out.

It is possible to locate in a plane (a two-dimensional space) three points, and only three, whose mutual distances are equal. This mathematical fact finds graphic expression in the equilateral triangle. (A, Figure 1).

In three-dimensional, or solid space, it is possible to add a point, and the mutual equal distances, six

15

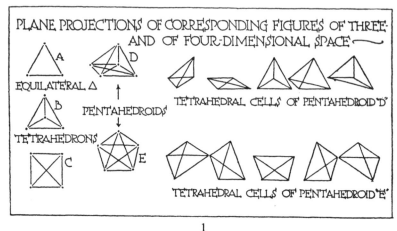

PLANE PROJECTIONS OF CORRESPONDING FIGURES OF THREE- AND OF FOUR-DIMENSIONAL SPACE

EQUILATERAL △ A

PENTAHEDROIDS D

TETRAHEDRONS B

TETRAHEDRAL CELLS OF PENTAHEDROID 'D'

C E

TETRAHEDRAL CELLS OF PENTAHEDROID 'E'

1

in number, between the four points, will be expressed by the edges of a regular tetrahedron whose vertices are the four points. But in order to represent this solid in a plane, we must have recourse to projective geometry. The most simple and obvious way to do this is to locate the fourth point in the center of the equilateral triangle and draw lines from this central point to the three vertices. Then we have a representation of a regular tetrahedron as seen directly from above, the central point representing the apex opposite the base (B, Figure 1). But suppose we imagine the tetrahedron to be *tilted* far enough over for this upper apex to fall (in plane projection) *outside* of the equilateral triangle representing the base. In such a position the latter would foreshorten to an isosceles triangle, and at a certain stage of this motion the plane projection of the tetrahedron appears as a square, its every apex representing an apex of the tetrahedron, whose edges are represented by the sides and diagonals of the square (C,

16

Figure 1). In this representation, though the points are equidistant on a plane, as they are equidistant in solid space, the six lines are not of the same length, and the four triangles are no longer truly equilateral. But this is owing to the exigencies of representation on a surface. If we imagine that we are not looking *at* a plane figure, but *into* a solid, the necessary corrections are made automatically by the mind, and we have no difficulty in identifying the figure as a tetrahedron.

Now if we concede to space another independent direction, in that *fourth dimension* we can add *another* point equidistant from all four vertices of the tetrahedron. The mutual distances between these *five* points will be ten in number and all equal. The *hyper*solid formed—a pentahedroid—will be bounded by five equal tetrahedrons in the same way that a tetrahedron is bounded by four equal equilateral triangles, and each of these by three equal lines. We cannot construct this figure, for to do so would require a space of four dimensions, but we can represent it in plane projection, just as we are able to represent a tetrahedron. We have only to add another point and connect it by lines with every point representing an apex of the original tetrahedron (D, Figure 1); or according to our second method we can arrange five points in such fashion as to coincide with the vertices of a regular pentagon and connect every one with every other one by means of straight lines (E, Figure 1). In either case by convention we have a plane representation of a hypertetrahedron or pentahedroid.

If we have really achieved the plane representation of a pentahedroid, it should be easy to identify the projections of the five tetrahedral cells or bounding tetrahedrons, just as we are able to identify the four equilateral sides of the tetrahedron in plane projection. We find that it is possible to do this. For convenience of identification, these are separately shown. By dint of continued gazing at this pentagon circumscribing a five-pointed star, and by trying to recognize all its intricate inter-relations, we may come finally to the feeling that it is not merely a figure on a plane, but that it represents a hypersolid of hyperspace, related to the tetrahedron as that is related to the triangle.

THE CORRESPONDING HIGHER DEVELOPMENTS OF THE SQUARE

Let us next consider the series beginning with the square. The cube may be conceived of as developed by the movement of a square in a direction at right angles to its two dimensions, a distance equal to the length of one of its sides. The direction of this movement can be *represented* on a plane anywhere we wish. Suppose we establish it as diagonally downward and to the right. The resultant figure is a cube in isometric perspective, for each of the four

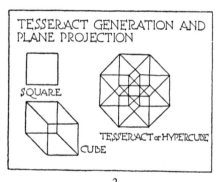

2

18

points has traced out a line, and each line has developed a (foreshortened) square (Figure 2). The mind easily identifies the figure as a cube, notwithstanding the fact that the sides are not all squares, that the angles are not all equal, and that the edges are not all mutually perpendicular.

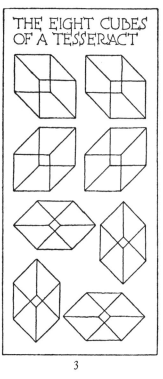

THE EIGHT CUBES OF A TESSERACT

3

Next let us, in thought, develop a hypercube, or tesseract. To do this it will be necessary to conceive of a cube as moving into the fourth dimension a distance equal to the length of one of its sides. For plane representation we can, as before, assume this direction to be anywhere we like. Let it be diagonally downward, to the left. In this position we draw a second cube, to represent the first at the end of its motion into the fourth dimension. And because each point has traced out a line, each line a square, and each square a cube, we must connect by lines all the vertices of the first cube with the corresponding vertices of the second. The resultant figure will be a perspective of a tesseract, or rather the perspective of a perspective, for it is a two-dimensional representation of a three-dimensional representation of a four-dimensional form (Figure 2).

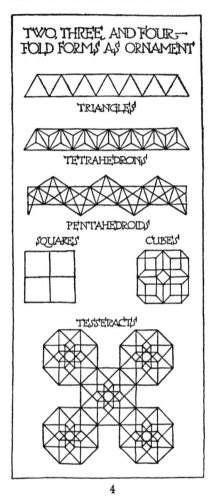

TWO, THREE, AND FOUR-FOLD FORMS AS ORNAMENT

TRIANGLES

TETRAHEDRONS

PENTAHEDROIDS

SQUARES   CUBES

TESSERACTS

4

If we have achieved the plane projection of a tesseract we should be able to identify the eight cubes by which it is bounded—the two at the beginning and end of the motion, and the six developed by the movement of the six faces of the cube into four-dimensional space. We find that we can do this. For convenience of identification the eight cubes are separately shown in Figure 3.

TRUTH TO THE MIND IS
BEAUTY TO THE EYE.

Ornament is largely a matter of the arrangement and repetition of a few well chosen motifs. The basis of ornament is geometry. If we arrange these various geometrical figures in sequence and in groups we have the rudiments of ornament (Figure 4). Although all these are plane figures, there is this important difference between them: the triangle and the square speak to the mind only in terms of two dimen-

20

sions; the plane representations of the tetrahedron and the cube portray certain relations in solid space, while those of the pentahedroid and the tesseract portray relations peculiar to four-dimensional space.

It will be observed that the decorative value of the figures increases as they proceed from space to space: the higher-dimensional developments are more beautiful and carry a greater weight of meaning. This accords well with the dictum, "Beauty is Truth; Truth, Beauty."

The above exercises constitute the only clue needed to understand the system of ornament here illustrated. Every symmetrical plane figure has its three-dimensional correlative, to which it is related as a boundary or a cross-section.

Tetrahedrons: Prisms

These solids may in turn be conceived of as boundaries or cross-sections of corresponding figures in four-dimensional space. The plane projections of these hypersolids are the motifs mainly used in Projective Ornament.

21

IV

THREE REGULAR POLYHEDROIDS

The paradoxes of four-dimensional geometry are best understood by referring them to the corresponding truisms of plane and of solid geometry. This may profitably be done in the case of the pentahedroid, the tesseract, and the 16-hedroid, the four-fold figures of most use in Projective Ornament. In the plane representation of four-fold figures for decorative purposes certain conventions should be observed, conventions which, though they serve aesthetic ends, find justification in optical and physical laws.

TWO-, THREE-, AND FOUR-FOLD FIGURES

THE most effective method for a novice to approach an understanding of any four-dimensional figure can be compared to the athletic exercise called the hop, skip and jump. In this the cumulative impetus given by the hop and the skip is concentrated and expended in the supreme effort of the jump. The jump into the fourth dimension is best prepared for, in any given case, by a preliminary hop in plane space, and a skip in solid space.

In the following cursory consideration of the three simplest regular polyhedroids of four-dimensional space let us apply this method. Even at the risk of wearisome reiteration let us resolve the paradoxes of hyperspace by referring them to the truisms of lower spaces.

A regular poly*gon*—a two-fold figure—consists of equal straight lines so joined as to enclose symmetrically a portion of *plane space.* A regular polyhe*dron* a three-fold figure—consists of a number of equal regular polygons, together with their interiors, the polygons being joined by their edges so as to enclose symmetrically a portion of *solid space*. A regular

polyhe*droid* consists of a number of equal regular polyhedrons, together with their interiors, the polyhedrons being joined by their faces so as to enclose symmetrically a portion of *hyperspace*.

In the foregoing chapter we have considered the two simplest regular polyhedroids: the regular pentahedroid, or hypertetrahedron, and the tesseract, or hypercube. To these let us now add the hexadekahedroid, or 16-hedroid, bounded by 16-tetrahedrons. These regular hypersolids are of such importance

Octahedrons: Tetrahedrons

in Projective Ornament that their elements should be familiar, and their construction understood.

THE PENTAHEDROID

A regular pentahedroid is a regular figure of four-dimensional space bounded by five regular tetrahedrons: it has five vertices, ten edges, ten faces, and five cells.

If we take an equilateral triangle and draw a line through its center perpendicular to its plane, every point of this line will be equidistant from the three vertices of the triangle, and if we take for a fourth vertex that point on this line whose distance from the three vertices is equal to one of the sides of the triangle, we have then a tetrahedron in which the edges are all equal.

If through the center of this regular tetrahedron we could draw a line perpendicular to its *hyper*plane every point of this line would be similarly, as above, equidistant from the four vertices of the tetrahedron, and we could take for a fifth vertex a point at a distance from the four vertices equal to one of the edges of the tetrahedron. We would have then a pentahedroid in which the ten edges would all be equal.

Tetrahedrons: Icosahedrons

All the parts of any one kind—face angles, dihedral angles, faces, etc.—would be equal; for the pentahedroid is congruent to itself in sixty different ways and can be made to coincide with itself, any part coinciding with any other part of the same kind.

As every regular polyhedroid can be inscribed in a hypersphere in the same way that a regular polygon can be inscribed in a circle, and every regular polyhedron in a sphere, the pentahedroid is most truly represented in plane projection as inscribed within a circle representing this hypersphere. Radii perpendicular to the cells of the pentahedroid meet the hypersphere in five points which are the vertices of a second regular pentahedroid symmetrically situated to the first with respect to the center, and therefore equal to the first. Representing these vertices by equidistant intermediate points on the circle circumscribing the pentahedroid and completing the figure, we have a graphic representation of this fact (Figure 5). These

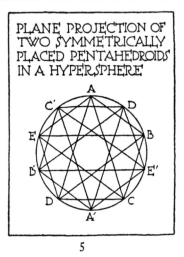

PLANE PROJECTION OF TWO SYMMETRICALLY PLACED PENTAHEDROIDS IN A HYPERSPHERE

5

intersecting pentahedroids inscribed within a hypersphere have their analogue in plane space in two symmetrically intersecting equilateral triangles inscribed within a circle, and in solid space in two symmetrical intersecting tetrahedrons inscribed within a sphere (Figure 6).

THE TESSERACT

The tesseract, or hypercube, is a regular figure of four-dimensional space having eight cubical cells, twenty-four square faces, (each a common face of two cubes), thirty-two equal edges, and sixteen vertices. It contains four axes lying in lines which also form a rectangular system.

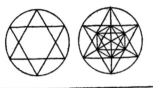

DOUBLE EQUILATERAL TRIANGLE IN A CIRCLE & DOUBLE TETRAHEDRON IN A SPHERE.

6

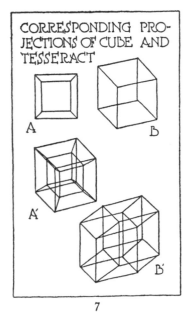

CORRESPONDING PROJECTIONS OF CUBE AND TESSERACT

A   B

A'   B'

7

In order to comprehend the tesseract in plane representation, let us first consider the corresponding plane representation of the cube. In parallel perspective a cube appears as a square inside of another square, with oblique lines connecting the four vertices (A, Figure 7). By reason of our tactile and visual experience, the inner and smaller square is thought of as the same size as the outer and larger, and the four intermediate quadrilateral figures are thought of as squares also. If the cube is shown not in parallel, but oblique perspective, the mind easily identifies the two figures (B, Figure 7).

These two ways of representing a cube in plane space may be followed in the case of the tesseract also (A' and B', Figure 7). We can think of the first as representing the appearance of the tesseract as we look down into it, and the second as we stand a little to one side. In each case it is possible to identify the eight cubes whose interiors form the cells of

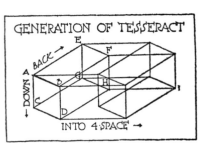

GENERATION OF TESSERACT

8

the tesseract. The fact that they are not cubes except by convention is owing to the exigencies of representation: in four-dimensional space the cells are perfect cubes, and are correlated into a figure whose four dimensions are all equal.

In order to familiarize ourselves with this, for our purposes the most important of all four-fold figures, let us again consider the manner of its generation, beginning with the point. Let the point A, Figure 8, move to the right, terminating with the point B. Next let the line AB move downward a distance equal to its length, tracing out the square AD.

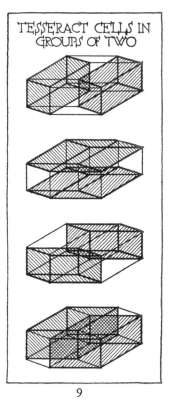

TESSERACT CELLS IN GROUPS OF TWO

9

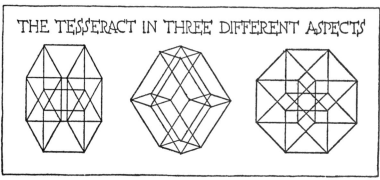

THE TESSERACT IN THREE DIFFERENT ASPECTS

10

29

This square shall now move backward the same distance, generating the (stretched out) cube A H. And now, having exhausted the three mutually perpendicular directions of solid space, and undaunted by the physical impracticability of the thing, let this cube move off in a direction perpendicular to its every dimension (the fourth dimension) *represented* by the arrow. This will generate the tesseract A I. It will be found to contain eight cubical cells. For convenience of identification these are shown in Figure 9. Other aspects of the tesseract are shown in Figure 10; and in Figure 11 it is shown with an intermediate or cross-sectional square in each of the cubes, which square in the tesseract becomes an intermediate cube. Whenever, in the figure, we have three squares in the same straight line, we know that we have a cube. There are eight of these groups of three, the cubical cells of the tesseract. If instead of representing the fourth direction *outside* the generating cube we choose to conceive of it as *inward*, the resultant figure is that shown at the bot-

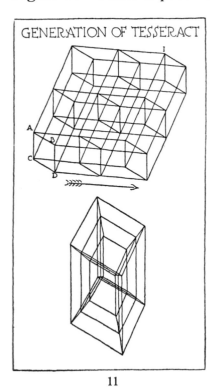

GENERATION OF TESSERACT

11

30

tom of Figure 11, the innermost of these cubes corresponding with the furthermost of the upper figure.

THE 16-HEDROID

After the pentahedroid or hypertetrahedron, and the tesseract or hypercube, already considered, we have as the next regular polyhedroid the hexadekahedroid, or, more briefly, the 16-hedroid.

If we lay off a given distance in both directions on each of four mutually perpendicular lines intersecting at a point, the eight points so obtained are the vertices of a regular polyhedroid which has four diagonals along the four given lines. This is the 16-hedroid. It has, as the name implies, sixteen cells, (each a tetrahedron), thirty-two triangular faces, (each face common to two tetrahedrons), twenty-four edges, and eight vertices.

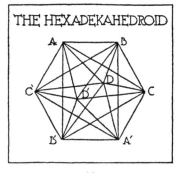

12

Figure 12 represents its projection upon a plane. The sixteen cells are ABCD, A′B′C′D′, AB′C′D′, A′BCD, AB′CD, A′BC′D, ABC′D, A′B′CD′, ABCD′, A′B′C′D, ABC′D′, A′B′CD, A′BC′D, AB′CD′, A′BCD′, AB′C′D. The accented letters are the antipodes of the unaccented ones. Figure 13 represents another plane projection of this polyhedroid.

THE DECORATIVE VALUE OF THESE FIGURES

As this is a handbook for artists and not a geometrical treatise, the description of regular polyhedroids need not be carried further than this. The reader who is ambitious to continue, from the 24-hedroid even unto the 600-hedroid, is referred to the geometry of four dimensions; upon this he can exercise his mind and experience for himself the stern joy of the conquest of new spaces. But the designer has already, in the pentahedroid, the hypercube, and the hexadekahedroid, ample material on which to exercise his skill. It should be remembered that just as in plane geometry a regular polygon can always be inscribed in a circle, and in geometry of three dimensions a regular polyhedron can always be inscribed in a sphere, so in four-dimensional geometry every regular polyhedroid can be inscribed in a hypersphere. In plane projection this hypersphere would be represented by a circle circumscribing the plane figure representing the polyhedroid.

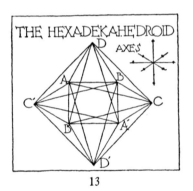

THE HEXADEKAHEDROID

13

Almost any random arrangement on the page of these three hypersolids in plane projection will serve to indicate what largess of beauty is here—they are like cut jewels, like flowers, and like frost. Combined symmetrically they form patterns of endless variety.

THE CONVENTIONS EMPLOYED IN THEIR REPRESENTATION

There is a reason why the plane projections of hypersolids are shown as transparent. Our senses operate two-dimensionally—that is, we see and contact only surfaces. Were our sense mechanism truly three-dimensional, we should have X-ray vision, and the surfaces of solids would offer no resistance to the touch. In dealing with four-dimensional space we are at liberty to imagine ourselves in full possession of this augmented power of sight and touch. The mind having ascended into the fourth dimension, there would follow a corresponding augmentation on the part of the senses, by reason of which the interiors of solids would be as open as are the interiors of plane figures.

There is justification also for the attenuation of all lines towards their center. It is in obedience to the optical law that when the light is behind an object it so impinges upon the intercepting object as to produce the effect of a thinning towards the center. The actual form of the bars of a leaded glass window, for example, is as shown in A, Figure 14, but their optical effect when seen against the light is as in B. Because in X-ray vision some substances are opaque, and some translucent, we are at liberty to attribute opacity to any part

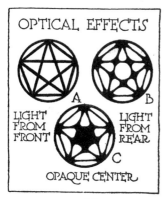

OPTICAL EFFECTS

A

B

LIGHT FROM FRONT

LIGHT FROM REAR

C

OPAQUE CENTER

14

we please, and thus to add a new factor of variation as in C. We are also at liberty to stretch, twist or shear the figures in any manner we like. By the use of tones, of color, or by mitigating the crystalline rigidity of the figures through their combination with floral forms, we can create a new ornamental mode well adapted to the needs of today.

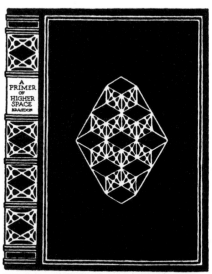

BINDING A TESSERACT OF STRETCHED 3-CUBES

V

FOLDING DOWN

Regular polyhedroids of four-dimensional space may be unfolded in three-dimensional space, and these again unfolded in a space of two-dimensions; or, contrariwise, they may be built up by assembling the regular polyhedrons which compose them. In this way new and valuable decorative material is obtained.

ANOTHER METHOD OF REPRESENTING THE HIGHER IN THE LOWER

THE perspective method is not the only one whereby four-fold figures may be represented in three-dimensional and in two-dimensional space. Polyhedroids may be conceived of as cut apart along certain *planes*, and folded down into three-dimensional space in a manner analogous to that by which a cardboard box may be cut along certain of its *edges* and folded down into a plane. As the boundaries of a polyhedroid are polyhedrons, an unfolded polyhedroid will consist of a number of related polyhedrons. These can in turn be unfolded, and the aggregation of polygons—each a plane boundary of the solid boundary of a hypersolid—will represent a four-fold figure unfolded in a space of two dimensions.

An unfolded cube becomes a cruciform plane figure, made up of six squares, each one a boundary of the cube (A, Figure 15). Similarly, if we imagine a tesseract to be unfolded, its eight cubical cells will occupy three-dimensional space in the shape of a double-armed cross (B, Figure 15). In four-dimensional space these cubes can be turned in upon one another to form a symmetrical figure just as in three-dimensional space the six squares can be re-united to form a cube.

A regular tetrahedron unfolded yields an equilateral triangle enclosed by three other equilateral triangles (C, Figure 15). Similarly, an unfolded pentahedroid, or hyper tetrahedron, would consist of a central tetrahedron with four others resting on its four faces (D, Figure 15). The pentahedroid could be re-formed by turning these towards one another in four-dimensional space, until they came completely together again.

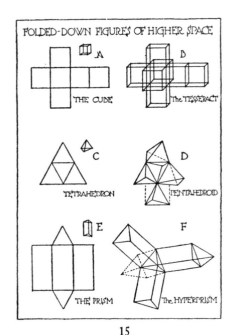

FOLDED-DOWN FIGURES OF HIGHER SPACE

A — THE CUBE
B — The TESSERACT
C — TETRAHEDRON
D — PENTAHEDROID
E — THE PRISM
F — The HYPERPRISM

15

A regular triangular prism unfolded yields three parallelograms, its sides; and two equilateral triangles, its ends (E, Figure 15). Similarly, a regular hyperprism would unfold into four equal and similar triangular prisms and two tetrahedrons (F, Figure 15). In four-dimensional space we could turn these prisms around the faces of the tetrahedron upon which they rest and the other tetrahedron around the face by which it is attached to one of the prisms, and bring them all together, each prism with a lateral face resting upon a lateral face of each of the others, and each of the four faces of the second tetrahedron resting upon one of the prisms. This could be done without separating any of the figures, or distorting them in any way, and the figure thus folded up would then enclose completely a portion of four-dimensional space.

THE POLYHEDRAL BOUNDARIES OF FOUR-DIMENSIONAL REGULAR ANGLES

A regular angle for any dimensional space is one all of whose boundaries are the same in form and magnitude. The summits of all regular figures in any space form regular angles since the distribution of their boundaries is symmetrical and equal. G and H, Figure 16, represent respectively the summits, one in each figure, of the tetrahedron and the cube, with the two-dimensional boundaries of the summit spread out symmetrically in a plane. The boundaries of the summits of a four-dimensional figure being solids, G' and H' represent respectively the summits, one in each figure, of the higher correlatives of the

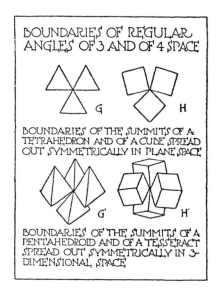

BOUNDARIES OF REGULAR ANGLES OF 3 AND OF 4 SPACE

G   H

BOUNDARIES OF THE SUMMITS OF A TETRAHEDRON AND OF A CUBE SPREAD OUT SYMMETRICALLY IN PLANE SPACE

G'   H'

BOUNDARIES OF THE SUMMITS OF A PENTAHEDROID AND OF A TESSERACT SPREAD OUT SYMMETRICALLY IN 3-DIMENSIONAL SPACE

16

tetrahedron and the cube—the pentahedroid and the tesseract—spread out in three-dimensional space. That is, they represent, in three-dimensional perspective, the symmetrical arrangement of the four boundaries of regular four-dimensional angles. In four-dimensional space the faces of those figures which lie adjacent to the common vertex are brought into coincidence, just as in three-dimensional space the *edges* of the triangles and squares adjacent to the common vertex are brought into coincidence, forming the summits of the tetrahedron and the cube.

THE CONSTRUCTION OF THE 24-HEDROID

It is possible to build up any regular polyhedroid by putting together a set of polyhedrons. We take them in succession in such order that each is joined to those already taken by a set of polygons like the incomplete polyhedron.

Take the case of the four-fold icositetrahedroid or 24-hedroid. I, Figure 17, shows a summit with six octahedral boundaries arranged about it symmetrically in three-dimensional space. Conceive I to be transported into four-dimensional space, and the interstices between the adjacent triangular faces to be closed up by joining those faces two and two; the figure assumes a form whose projection is represented in J with dotted lines omitted. Adjust to this figure twelve other octahedrons in a symmetrical manner; three of these octahedrons are represented by the dotted lines of J. Again, close up the interstices between the adjacent faces; the outline of the figure assumes a form whose projection is represented in K.

40

Now conceive this figure to be turned inside out. There will be left in the middle of the figure a vacant space of exactly the form of J with the dotted lines omitted (L, Figure 17): such a group of six octahedrons is therefore required to complete the four-fold figure. By counting it is found that all the constituent octahedral summits of the four-fold figure are filled to saturation, and that the figure is in other respects complete and regular. The number of octahedral boundaries or cells is twenty-four; of summits, twenty-four; of triangular faces, ninety-six; of edges, ninety-six.

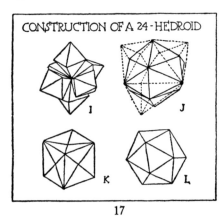

CONSTRUCTION OF A 24-HEDROID

I   J

K   L

17

TESSERACT SECTIONS

In the same way that it is easy to conceive all regular polygons as two-dimensional boundaries or cross-sections of regular polyhedrons, it is possible, though not so easy, to conceive of these same polygons as boundaries or cross-sections of corresponding polyhedroids.

The various figures are represented in perspective projection, but they may be unfolded, after the manner of the cardboard box. If this be done the bounding polygons will be free from the distortions incident to perspective representation, but the result

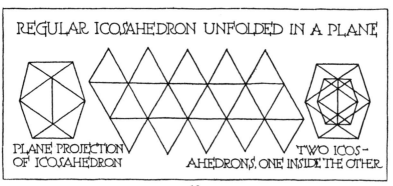

REGULAR ICOSAHEDRON UNFOLDED IN A PLANE

PLANE PROJECTION OF ICOSAHEDRON

TWO ICOS - AHEDRONS, ONE INSIDE THE OTHER

18

in most cases is the monotonous and uninteresting repetition of units (Figure 18). What we require for ornament is greater contrast and variety of form, and this may be obtained without going farther than the wonder-box of the tesseract itself.

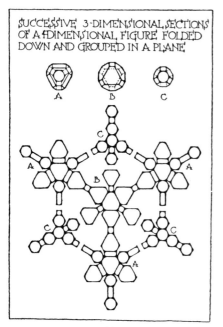

SUCCESSIVE 3-DIMENSIONAL SECTIONS OF A 4-DIMENSIONAL FIGURE FOLDED DOWN AND GROUPED IN A PLANE

19

There are certain interesting polyhedroids embedded, as it were, in the tesseract. Such are the tetratesseract, and the octatesseract. This last is obtained by cutting off every corner of the tesseract just as an octahedron is left if every corner of a cube is cut off. Three such polyhedral sections of a tesseract, unfolded, repeated, and arranged symmetrically with relation to one another, produce the highly decorative pattern shown in Figure 19.

BINDING: FOUR TESSERACTS AND FOUR CUBES

VI

MAGIC LINES IN MAGIC SQUARES

The numerical harmony inherent in magic squares finds graphic expression in the magic lines which may be traced in them. These lines, translated into ornament, yield patterns often of amazing richness and variety, beyond the power of the unaided aesthetic sense to compass. Magic lines have relations to spaces higher than a plane—they, too, are Projective Ornament.

THE HISTORY OF MAGIC SQUARES

ALMOST everyone knows what a magic square is. Briefly, it is a numerical acrostic, an arrangement of numbers in the form of a square, which, when added in vertical and horizontal rows and along the diagonals, yield the same sum. Magic squares are of Eastern and ancient origin. There is a magic square of 4 carved in Sanskrit characters on the gate of the fort at Gwalior, in India (Figure 20). Engraved on stone and metal, magic squares are worn at the present day in the East as talismans or amulets. They are known to have occupied the attention of Mediaeval philosophers, astrologers, and mystics. Albrecht Dürer introduced what is perhaps the most remarkable of all magic squares into his etching *Melencolia I* (Figure 21). Today they find place in the puzzle departments of magazines. Their laws and formulas have engaged the serious attention of eminent mathematicians, and the discovery of so-called magical relations between numbers, not alone in squares, but in cubes and hyper-cubes, is one of the recreations of the science of mathematics.*

The artist, impatient of concept, but questing the beautiful, will care little about the mathematical aspect of the matter, but it should interest him to know that the magic lines of magic squares are rich in decorative possibilities.

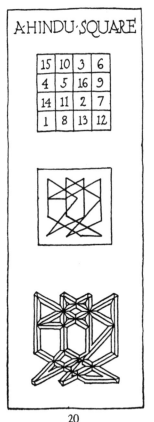

A·HINDU·SQUARE

15	10	3	6
4	5	16	9
14	11	2	7
1	8	13	12

20

A magic line is that endless line formed by following the numbers of a magic square in their natural sequence from cell to cell and returning to the point of departure. Because most magic squares are developed by arranging the numbers in their natural order in the form of a square and then subjecting them to certain *rotations*, the whole thing may be compared to the formation of string figures—the cat's cradle of one's childhood—in which a loop of string is made to assume various intricate and often amazing patterns—*magic lines in space.*

*See Philip Henry Wynne's Magic Tesseract in the author's Primer of Higher Space.

THEIR FORMATION

Without going at all deeply into the arcana of the subject it will not be amiss to suggest one of the methods of magic square formation by the simplest possible example, the magic square of 3. Arrange the digits in sequence in three horizontal lines, and relate them to the cells of a square as shown in Figure 22. This will leave four cells empty

21

and four numbers outside the perimeter. Dispose these numbers, not in the empty cells which they adjoin, but in the ones opposite; in other words, rotate the outside numbers in a direction at right angles to the plane of the paper, about the lines which

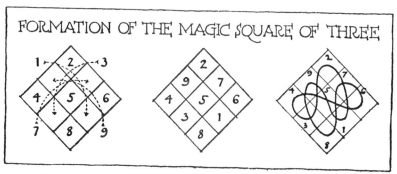

FORMATION OF THE MAGIC SQUARE OF THREE

22

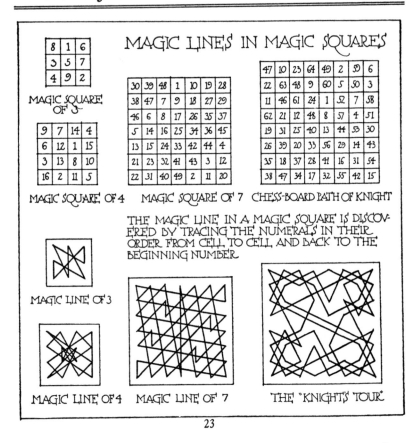

MAGIC LINES IN MAGIC SQUARES

8	1	6
3	5	7
4	9	2

MAGIC SQUARE OF 3

9	7	14	4
6	12	1	15
3	13	8	10
16	2	11	5

MAGIC SQUARE OF 4

30	39	48	1	10	19	28
38	47	7	9	18	27	29
46	6	8	17	26	35	37
5	14	16	25	34	36	45
13	15	24	33	42	44	4
21	23	32	41	43	3	12
22	31	40	49	2	11	20

MAGIC SQUARE OF 7

47	10	23	64	49	2	59	6
22	63	48	9	60	5	50	3
11	46	61	24	1	52	7	58
62	21	12	48	8	57	4	51
19	31	25	40	13	44	53	30
26	39	20	33	56	29	14	43
35	18	37	28	41	16	31	54
38	47	34	17	32	55	42	15

CHESS-BOARD PATH OF KNIGHT

THE MAGIC LINE IN A MAGIC SQUARE IS DISCOV-
ERED BY TRACING THE NUMERALS IN THEIR
ORDER FROM CELL TO CELL AND BACK TO THE
BEGINNING NUMBER

MAGIC LINE OF 3

MAGIC LINE OF 4

MAGIC LINE OF 7

THE "KNIGHT'S TOUR"

23

severally bound the central cell. By this operation
each outside number will fall in its proper place.
These rotations are indicated by dotted lines. The
result is the magic square of 3. Each line, in each
of the two dimensions of the square, adds to 15,
and the two diagonals yield the same sum.

Now with a pencil, using a free-hand curve,
follow the numbers in their order from 1 to 9 and
back again to 1. The result is the magic line of the

magic square of 3 (Figure 22). We have here a configuration of great beauty and interest, readily translatable into ornament. As the number of magic squares is practically infinite, and as each contains a magic line, here is a rich field for the designer, even though not all magic lines lend them selves to decorative treatment. Figures 23 and 24, show some of them which do so lend themselves, and Figures 25, 26 and 27 show the translation of a few of these into ornament.

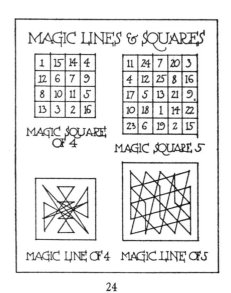

24

THE KNIGHT'S TOUR

It is a common feat of chess players to make the tour of the board by the knight's move (two squares forward and one to right or left), starting at any

25

square, touching at each square once, and returning to the point of departure. Keller, the magician, introduced this trick into his performance, permitting any member of the audience to designate the initial square.

PATTERN FROM MAGIC SQUARES

MAGIC LINE FROM A SQUARE OF 5

MAGIC LINE OF 3 TAKEN FOUR TIMES

PATH TRACED BY THE KNIGHT IN MAKING WHAT IS KNOWN AS THE "KNIGHT'S TOUR"

26

It is a simple feat of mnemonics. The performer must remember 64 numbers in their order, the sequence which yields the magic line in the magic square of 8. The plotting of this line is shown in Figure 23; its decorative application in the binding of *The Beautiful Necessity.* Euler, the great mathematician, constructed knight's move squares of 5 and of 6, having peculiar properties. In one diagram of Figure 28 the natural numbers show the path of a knight moving in such a manner that the sum of the pairs of numbers opposite to and equidistant from the middle figure is its double. In the other diagram the knight returns to its starting cell in such a manner that the difference between the pairs of numbers opposite to and equidistant from the middle point is 18.

MAGIC LINE OF 7

27

INTERLACES

Figure 28 shows interlaces derived from these two magic squares. They so resemble the braided bands found on Celtic crosses that one

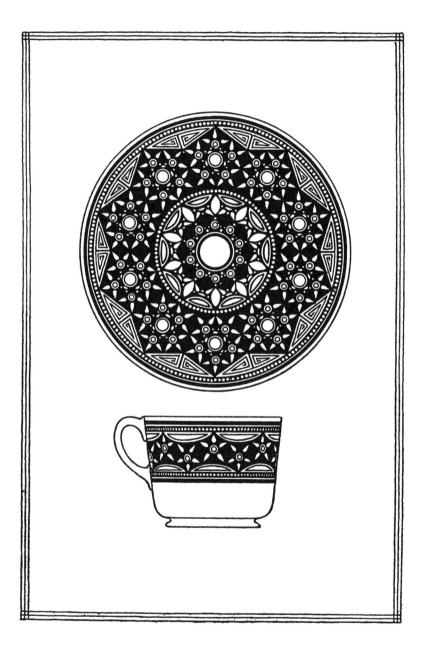

EULER'S KNIGHT'S-TOUR SQUARES

23	18	11	6	25
10	5	24	17	12
19	22	13	4	7
14	9	2	21	16
1	20	15	8	3

30	21	6	15	28	19
7	16	29	20	5	14
22	31	8	35	18	27
9	36	17	26	13	4
32	23	2	11	34	25
1	10	33	24	3	12

MAGIC LINES FROM EULER'S SQUARES

28

naturally wonders if their unknown and admirable artists may not have possessed the secret of deriving ornament from magic numerical arrangements, for these arrangements are not limited to the square, but embrace polygons of every description. Here is another curious fact in this connection:

Albrecht Dürer, whose acquaintance with magic squares is a matter of record, is known to have expended a part of his inventive genius in designing interlacing knots. Leonardo da Vinci also amused himself in this way. The element of the mystic and mysterious entered into the genius of both these masters of the Renaissance. One wonders if this may not have been due to some secret affiliation with an occult fraternity of adepts, whose existence and claims to the possession of extraordinary knowledge and power have

PATTERNS FROM EULER'S KNIGHTS-MOVE SQUARES

29

been the subject of much debate. Were these knots of theirs not only ornaments, but symbols—password and counter-sign pointing to knowledge not possessed by the generality of men?

These patterns show forth in graphic form the symphonic harmony which abides in mathematics, a fact of sweeping significance, inasmuch as it involves the philosophical problem of the world-order. The same order that prevails in these figures permeates the universe; through them one may sense the cosmic harmony of the spheres, just as it is possible to hear the ocean in a shell.

THE PROJECTED MAGIC LINE

In answer to any question which may arise in the mind of the reader as to the relevancy of magic squares to the subject of Projective Ornament, it may be stated that magic lines are Projective Ornament in a very strict sense. These lines, though figures on a plane, represent an extension

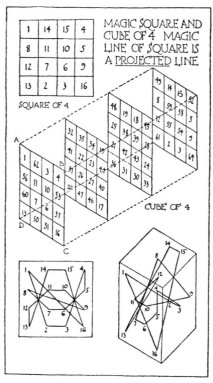

MAGIC SQUARE AND CUBE OF 4 MAGIC LINE OF SQUARE IS A PROJECTED LINE

30

tion at right angles to the plane, and they have relations to the third and higher dimensions. As this is a fact of considerable interest and importance, the attempt will be made to carry its demonstration at least far enough to assure the reader of its substantial truth. Let us examine the three-dimensional aspect of the magic line in a magic square of 4.

Figure 30 represents one of the most remarkable magic squares. Each horizontal, each vertical and each diagonal column adds 34. The four corner cells add 34, and the four central cells add 34. The two middle cells of the top row add 34 with the two middle cells of the bottom row. The middle cells of the right and left columns similarly add 34. Go round the square clock-wise; the first cell beyond the first corner, plus the first beyond the second corner, plus the third, plus the fourth, equals 34. Take any number at random, find the three other numbers corresponding to it in any manner that respects symmetrically two dimensions, and the sum of the numbers is 34.

In Figure 30 is also represented the magic cube of 4. It is made up of 64 cubical cells, each containing one of the numbers from 1 to 64, inclusive. This cube can be sliced into four vertical sections from left to right, or it can be separated into four other vertical sections by cutting planes perpendicular to the edge A B, proceeding from front to back, or the four sections may be horizontal, made by planes perpendicular to AD.

Now each of these twelve sections presents a magic square in which each row and each column adds 130. The diagonals of these squares do not

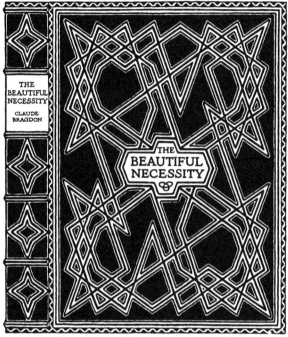

BINDING: THE KNIGHTS TOUR (MAGIC LINE OF 8-SQUARE)

add 130, but the four diagonals of the cube do add 130. The essential correspondence of the magic square of 4 to the magic cube of 4 is clearly apparent.

Now if we plot that portion of the magic line of the magic cube of 4 embraced by the numbers from 1 to 16 and compare it with the magic line of the magic square of 4, it is seen that the latter is a plane projection of the former.

In other words, shut the four sections of the cube up so that the front section, A C, in 1-16 fits over the back section, 49-64; then using only the numbers

57

1 to 16, they will be found to fall magically into the same places they occupy in the magic square of 4.

Because all magic lines in magic squares have, in their corresponding cubes, this three-dimensional extension, the patterns derived from magic squares come properly under the head of Projective Ornament.

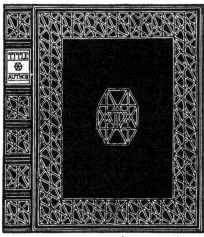

BINDING · THE MAGIC LINE OF 3. A TESSERACT

VII

A PHILOSOPHY OF ORNAMENT

The language of form is a symbolical expression of the world order. This order presents itself to individual consciousness most movingly and dramatically under the guise of fate and of free-will. For these two the straight line and the curve are graphic expressions. An ornamental mode should therefore embrace an intelligent and harmonious use of both. That Projective Ornament appears here so largely as a straight line system is because such a system is easier and more elementary than the other, and because this is an elementary treatise—merely a point of departure for an all-embracing art of the future, only to be developed by the coöperation of many minds.

THE WORLD ORDER AND THE WORD ORDER

PROJECTED solids and hypersolids, unfolded figures, magic lines in magic squares, these and similar translations of the truths of number into graphic form, are the words and syllables of the new ornamental mode. But we shall fail to develop a form language, eloquent and compelling, if we preoccupy ourselves solely with sources—the mere lexicography of ornament. There is a grammar and a rhetoric to be mastered as well. The words are not enough, there remains the problem of the word order.

Now the problem of the word order is the analogue of the problem of the world order. The sublime function of true art is to shadow forth the world order through any frail and fragmentary thing a man may make with his hands, so that the great thing can be sensed in the little, the permanent in

Cubes: Line in Magic Square of 3

the transitory, as the sun, for instance, is imaged in a dandelion, or a solar system in summer moths circling about a flame.

The world order and the word order alike obey the law of polar opposites. The hard and sibilant in sound, the rigid and flowing in form, correspond to opposite powers: the former to that kind, igneous, masculine, which resists, and the latter to the aqueous, feminine type which prevails by yielding; the first made the granite hills, the second, the fertile valleys. For these great opposites there are a thousand symbols: the cliff, the cloud; the oak, the vine—nature's "inevitable duality." One term corresponds to fate, destiny, and the other to free-will, forever forced to adjust itself to destiny. Each individual life, be it a Narcissus flower or a Napoleon, is the resultant of these two forces. The expansion of that life in space or on the field of action is determined by what we name its "star". In the case of the flower this is its invisible geometrical pattern to which the unfolding of every leaf and petal must conform; in the case of the man it is his destiny— his horoscope—the character with which he was born.

FATE AND FREE-WILL AND THEIR SYMBOLS

Here we have one of those universal truths, fixed from the foundation of the world. Fate decrees— "Thus far shalt thou go and no farther." Free-will whispers—"Within these limits thou art free." Music figures these two admonitions of the spirit in the key, the beat, the movement, which correspond to destiny; and in the melody, which with all its freedom conforms to the key, obeys the beat, and comes to its appointed end in the return of the dominant to the tonic at the end of the passage. To symbolize the same two elements in ornament, what is for the first more fitting than figures of geometry, because they are absolute and inexorable; and for the second, than the fecund and free-spreading forms of vegetable life?

Line in Magic Square of 8

Whether or not we choose to impute to geometrical and to floral forms the symbolical meaning here assigned them, we cannot fail to recognize these two elements in ornament, and a corresponding relation between them. There is the fixed frame or barrier, and there is the free-growing arabesque whose vigor faints against the crystalline rigidity of the frame—the diminishing energy returning upon itself in exquisite curves and spirals, like a wave from the face of a cliff. In the language of orna-

63

Tesseracts

ment, here is an expression of the highest spiritual truth—fate and free-will in perfect reconcilement. If from this point of view we consider even so hackneyed a thing as a Corinthian capital, the droop of the acanthus leaf where it meets the abacus becomes eloquent of that submission, after a life of effort, to a destiny beyond our failing energy to overpass. This exquisite acquiescence, expressed thus in terms of form, is capable of affecting the emotions as music does—

"That strain again, it hath a dying fall."

It is the beautiful end to tragedy, summed up in Hamlet's—

"But let it be.—Horatio, I am dead."

POLARITY

To create a new ornamental mode, we should conceive of ornament in this spirit, not as mere rhythmic space subdivision and flower conventionalization, but as symbology, most pregnant and profound. We must believe that form can teach as eloquently as the spoken word.

The artist is not committed to a slavish fidelity to the forms of nature. God of his own self-created world, he may fashion for it a flora all its own; but by the *laws* of nature he must be bound, for God himself, it has been said, is subject to the law of God.

Tesseracts

What is this law? "Male and female created he them," Genesis makes answer; and the Upanishads — "Brahma, that the world might be born, fell asunder into man and wife." Science says the same thing when it declares that the sundering of a force into two opposed activities striving for reunion, is a characteristic of all of the phenomena of nature, from magnet and crystal to man himself.

We begin to learn this law almost at birth; youth and maiden are learning it when they fall in love with one another, and philosophers, when adolescent fires die in the grate, are still engaged upon the same lesson. One Montessori exercise for very young children consists in providing them two boxes and a number of different geometrical solids made of wood, with instructions to put together in one box those forms that are angular, like the tetrahedron and the cube, and in the other those that are smooth to the touch, like the egg and the sphere. The artist, a child more knowing, in the schoolroom of the world, should set himself a similar task. Time and space are his two boxes; his assemblage of figures, all of the contents of consciousness and of the world.

PROJECTIVE ORNAMENT

SPACE AND TIME: THE FIELD AND THE FRAME

Now the characteristic of time is succession; in time alone one thing follows another in endless sequence. The unique characteristic of space is simultaneity, for in space alone everything exists at once. In classifying the arts, for example, music would go into the time box, for it is in time alone, being successive; architecture, on the other hand, would go into the space box. Yet because nothing is pure, so to speak, architecture has something of the element of succession, and music of simultaneousness. An arcade or a colonnade may be spoken of as successive; while a musical chord, consisting of several notes sounded together, is simultaneous.

The same thing holds true throughout nature. The time element and the space element everywhere appear, either explicitly or implicitly, the first as succession, the second as simultaneity.

In ornament we have the field and the frame, and the unfolding of living forms in space within some fixed time cycle may be thought of as symbolized by a foliated field and a geometrical frame or border. In the field, the units will be disposed with relation to points and radiating lines, implying the simultaneity of space, and in the border they will be arranged sequentially, implying the succession of time (Figure 31). Seeking greater interest, subtlety, and variety, we have, in the projected plane representations of symmetrical three-fold and four-fold solids, a frame rhythmically subdivided. These subdivisions of a frame may be taken to represent lesser time cycles within a greater, and the arabesque with which these spaces can be filled may be felt to

symbolize the growth of a plant through successive seasons, or the development of an individual in different incarnations.

A BOOK ALL BONES AND NO FLESH

It is by artifices such as these that the world order gets itself externalized in forms and arrangements which express "the life movement of the spirit through the rhythm of things." This is the very essence

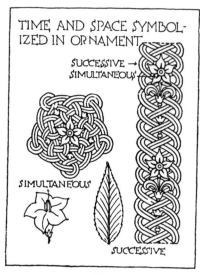

TIME AND SPACE SYMBOLIZED IN ORNAMENT

SUCCESSIVE →
SIMULTANEOUS

SIMULTANEOUS

SUCCESSIVE

31

of art: first to perceive, and then to publish news from that nowhere of the world from which all things flow and to which all things return. It will be evident to the discerning reader from what has been said regarding the symbolic value of the straight line and the curve (the frame and the arabesque) that the whole subject of foliated or free-spreading ornament has received scant attention from the author. This intentional concentration upon the straight line explains the poverty and hard monotony of many of the diagrams here presented. They are not so much ornament as the osseous framework of ornament. But by reason of our superficial manner of observing nature, our preoccupation with mere externals, we have lost our perception of her beautiful bones—her geometry. When we have recovered that, the rest is easy. It has seemed best not to complicate the subject nor confuse the issue, by proceeding to show (as one might) the relation of floral forms to geometrical figures, for this is something that every artist can look into for himself.

VIII

THE USES OF PROJECTIVE
ORNAMENT

Projective Ornament, being directly derived from geometry, is universal
in its nature. It is not a compendium of patterns, but a system for
the creation of patterns. Its principles are simple and comprehensive
and their application to particular problems stimulates and develops
the aesthetic sense, the mind, and the imagination.

THE FIELD AND FUNCTION OF PROJECTIVE ORNAMENT

PROJECTIVE Ornament is that rhythmic sub-division of space expressed through the figures
of Projective Geometry. As rhythmic space sub-
division is of the very essence of ornament, Projective Ornament possesses the element of univer-
sality, though it lends itself to some uses more
readily than to others. To those crafts which
employ linear design, such as lace-work, lead-work,
book-tooling, and the art of the jeweler, it is particu-
larly well suited; with color it lends itself admirably
to stained glass, textiles, and ceramics. On the
other hand, it must be considerably modified to
give to wrought iron an appropriate expression:
its application to cast iron and wood-inlaying presents fewer difficulties. Its three-dimensional, as
well as its two-dimensional aspects, come into play
in architecture, and from its many admirable geometrical forms there might be developed architectural
detail pleasing alike to the mind and to the eye. A
crying need of the time would thus be met. The drab

Hexadekahedroids

monotony of broad cement surfaces could be relieved by means of incrusted ornament in colored tiles arranged in patterns developed by the methods described.

Various applications of Projective Ornament to practical problems are suggested in the page illustrations dispersed throughout this volume, but a careful study of the text will be more profitable to the designer than any copying of the designs. If the rationale of the system is thoroughly grasped, a designer will no longer need to copy patterns, since he will have gained the power to create new ones for himself. To copy is the death of art. No worse fate could befall this book, or the person who would profit by it, than to use it merely as a book of patterns These should be looked upon only as illustrative of certain fundamental principles susceptible of endless application. Mr. Sullivan, from sad experience, predicted that the zeal of any converts that the book might make would be expended in sedulous imitation rather than in original creation. The author, however, takes a more hopeful view.

HOW TO AWAKEN THE SLEEPING BEAUTY

The principles here set forth are eminently communicable and understandable. They present no difficulty, even to an intelligent child. Indeed, the fashioning and folding up of elementary geometrical solids is a kindergarten exercise. The great impediment to success in this field is a proud and sophisticated mind. Let the learner "become as a little child," therefore: let him at all times exercise himself in Observational Geometry—that is, look for the simple geometrical forms and relations of the objects that come under his every-day notice. He should come to recognize that the myriad forms in the animal, vegetable, and mineral kingdoms furnish an unending variety of symmetrical and complex geometric forms which may be discovered and applied to his own problems. This should create an appetite for the study of Formal Geometry. From that study a fresh apprehension of the beauty of arithmetical relations is sure to follow. Enamored of this beauty, the disciple will seek out the basic geometrical ground rhythms latent in nature and in human life. The development of faculty will follow on the awakening of perception: the elements and relations grasped by the mind will externalize themselves in the work of the hand. Not content with the known and familiar space relationships, the student will essay to explore the

Hexadekahedroids

field of hyperspace. But let him not seek to achieve results too easily and too quickly. In all his work he should follow an orderly sequence, quarrying his gold before refining it, and fashioning it to his uses only after it is refined: that is, he should endeavor to understand the figures before he draws them, and he should draw them as geometrical diagrams before he attempts to alter and combine them for decorative use. It is the author's experience that they will require very little alteration; that they are in themselves decorative. The filling in of certain spaces for the purpose of achieving *notan* (contrast) is all that is usually required. This done, the application of color is the next step in the process: first comes line, then light and dark, and lastly color values. Such is the method of the Japanese, those masters of decorative design.

THE ILLUSTRATIONS AND DIAGRAMS

The black-and-white designs interspersed throughout the text represent Projective Ornament removed only one degree from geometrical diagrams, yet they are seen to be highly decorative even in this form. At the pleasure of the designer they may be elongated, contracted, sheared, twisted, translated from straight lines

into curves; and by subjecting them to these modi-
fications their beauty is often augmented. Yet if
their geometrical truth and integrity be too much
tampered with, they will be found to have lost a
certain precious quality. It would seem as though
they were beautiful to the eye in proportion as they

are interesting to the mind. For the sake of variety the figures are presented in three different ways; that is, in the form of *mons*, borders, and fields—corresponding to the point, the line, and the plane. It is clear that all-over patterns quite as interesting as those shown may be formed by repeating some of the unit figures. With this scant alphabet it is possible to spell more words than one or two.

Projective Ornament, derived as it is from Projective Geometry, is a new utterance of the transcendental truth of things. Whatever of beauty the figures in this book show forth has its source, not in any aesthetic idiosyncracy of the illustrator, but in that world order which number and geometry represent. These figures illustrate anew the idea, old as philosophy itself, that all forms are projections on the lighted screen of a material universe of archetypal ideas: that all of animate creation is one vast moving picture of the play of the Cosmic Mind. With the falling away of all our sophistries, this great truth will again startle and console mankind—that creation is beautiful and that it is necessitous, that the secret of beauty is necessity. "Let us build altars to the Beautiful Necessity."

CONCLUSION

Emerson says, "Perception makes. Perception has a destiny." How can new beauty be born into the world except by the awakening of new perception? Evolution is the master-key of modern science, but that very science ignores the evolution of consciousness—of perception. This it treats as

fixed, static. On the contrary, it is fluent, dynamic.
Were it not so, there would be little hope of a new art.
The modern mind has adventured far and fear-
lessly in the new realms of thought opened up by
research and discovery, but it has left no trail of
beauty. That it has not done so is the fault of the

artist, who has failed to interpret and portray the movement of the modern mind. Enamored of an outworn beauty, he has looked back, and like Lot's wife, he has become a pillar of salt. The outworn beauty is the beauty of mere *appearances*. The new beauty, which corresponds to the new knowledge, is the beauty of principles: not the world *aspect*, but the world *order*. The world order is most perfectly embodied in mathematics. This fact is recognized in a practical way by the scientist, who increasingly invokes the aid of mathematics. It should be recognized by the artist, and he should invoke the aid of mathematics too.

A CATALOG OF SELECTED
DOVER BOOKS
IN ALL FIELDS OF INTEREST

A CATALOG OF SELECTED DOVER
BOOKS IN ALL FIELDS OF INTEREST

DRAWINGS OF REMBRANDT, edited by Seymour Slive. Updated Lippmann, Hofstede de Groot edition, with definitive scholarly apparatus. All portraits, biblical sketches, landscapes, nudes. Oriental figures, classical studies, together with selection of work by followers. 550 illustrations. Total of 630pp. 9⅛ × 12¼.
21485-0, 21486-9 Pa., Two-vol. set $29.90

GHOST AND HORROR STORIES OF AMBROSE BIERCE, Ambrose Bierce. 24 tales vividly imagined, strangely prophetic, and decades ahead of their time in technical skill: "The Damned Thing," "An Inhabitant of Carcosa," "The Eyes of the Panther," "Moxon's Master," and 20 more. 199pp. 5⅜ × 8½. 20767-6 Pa. $3.95

ETHICAL WRITINGS OF MAIMONIDES, Maimonides. Most significant ethical works of great medieval sage, newly translated for utmost precision, readability. Laws Concerning Character Traits, Eight Chapters, more. 192pp. 5⅜ × 8½.
24522-5 Pa. $4.50

THE EXPLORATION OF THE COLORADO RIVER AND ITS CANYONS, J. W. Powell. Full text of Powell's 1,000-mile expedition down the fabled Colorado in 1869. Superb account of terrain, geology, vegetation, Indians, famine, mutiny, treacherous rapids, mighty canyons, during exploration of last unknown part of continental U.S. 400pp. 5⅜ × 8½. 20094-9 Pa. $7.95

HISTORY OF PHILOSOPHY, Julián Marías. Clearest one-volume history on the market. Every major philosopher and dozens of others, to Existentialism and later. 505pp. 5⅜ × 8½. 21739-6 Pa. $9.95

ALL ABOUT LIGHTNING, Martin A. Uman. Highly readable non-technical survey of nature and causes of lightning, thunderstorms, ball lightning, St. Elmo's Fire, much more. Illustrated. 192pp. 5⅜ × 8½. 25237-X Pa. $5.95

SAILING ALONE AROUND THE WORLD, Captain Joshua Slocum. First man to sail around the world, alone, in small boat. One of great feats of seamanship told in delightful manner. 67 illustrations. 294pp. 5⅜ × 8½. 20326-3 Pa. $4.95

LETTERS AND NOTES ON THE MANNERS, CUSTOMS AND CONDITIONS OF THE NORTH AMERICAN INDIANS, George Catlin. Classic account of life among Plains Indians: ceremonies, hunt, warfare, etc. 312 plates. 572pp. of text. 6⅛ × 9¼. 22118-0, 22119-9, Pa. Two-vol. set $17.90

ALASKA: The Harriman Expedition, 1899, John Burroughs, John Muir, et al. Informative, engrossing accounts of two-month, 9,000-mile expedition. Native peoples, wildlife, forests, geography, salmon industry, glaciers, more. Profusely illustrated. 240 black-and-white line drawings. 124 black-and-white photographs. 3 maps. Index. 576pp. 5⅜ × 8½. 25109-8 Pa. $11.95

CATALOG OF DOVER BOOKS

AMERICAN CLIPPER SHIPS: 1833–1858, Octavius T. Howe & Frederick C. Matthews. Fully-illustrated, encyclopedic review of 352 clipper ships from the period of America's greatest maritime supremacy. Introduction. 109 halftones. 5 black-and-white line illustrations. Index. Total of 928pp. 5⅜ × 8½.
25115-2, 25116-0 Pa., Two-vol. set $17.90

TOWARDS A NEW ARCHITECTURE, Le Corbusier. Pioneering manifesto by great architect, near legendary founder of "International School." Technical and aesthetic theories, views on industry, economics, relation of form to function, "mass-production spirit," much more. Profusely illustrated. Unabridged translation of 13th French edition. Introduction by Frederick Etchells. 320pp. 6⅛ × 9¼. (Available in U.S. only)
25023-7 Pa. $8.95

THE BOOK OF KELLS, edited by Blanche Cirker. Inexpensive collection of 32 full-color, full-page plates from the greatest illuminated manuscript of the Middle Ages, painstakingly reproduced from rare facsimile edition. Publisher's Note. Captions. 32pp. 9⅜ × 12¼.
24345-1 Pa. $4.95

BEST SCIENCE FICTION STORIES OF H. G. WELLS, H. G. Wells. Full novel *The Invisible Man*, plus 17 short stories: "The Crystal Egg," "Aepyornis Island," "The Strange Orchid," etc. 303pp. 5⅜ × 8½. (Available in U.S. only)
21531-8 Pa. $6.95

AMERICAN SAILING SHIPS: Their Plans and History, Charles G. Davis. Photos, construction details of schooners, frigates, clippers, other sailcraft of 18th to early 20th centuries—plus entertaining discourse on design, rigging, nautical lore, much more. 137 black-and-white illustrations. 240pp. 6⅛ × 9¼.
24658-2 Pa. $6.95

ENTERTAINING MATHEMATICAL PUZZLES, Martin Gardner. Selection of author's favorite conundrums involving arithmetic, money, speed, etc., with lively commentary. Complete solutions. 112pp. 5⅜ × 8½.
25211-6 Pa. $2.95

THE WILL TO BELIEVE, HUMAN IMMORTALITY, William James. Two books bound together. Effect of irrational on logical, and arguments for human immortality. 402pp. 5⅜ × 8½.
20291-7 Pa. $7.95

THE HAUNTED MONASTERY and THE CHINESE MAZE MURDERS, Robert Van Gulik. 2 full novels by Van Gulik continue adventures of Judge Dee and his companions. An evil Taoist monastery, seemingly supernatural events; overgrown topiary maze that hides strange crimes. Set in 7th-century China. 27 illustrations. 328pp. 5⅜ × 8½.
23502-5 Pa. $6.95

CELEBRATED CASES OF JUDGE DEE (DEE GOONG AN), translated by Robert Van Gulik. Authentic 18th-century Chinese detective novel; Dee and associates solve three interlocked cases. Led to Van Gulik's own stories with same characters. Extensive introduction. 9 illustrations. 237pp. 5⅜ × 8½.
23337-5 Pa. $4.95

Prices subject to change without notice.
Available at your book dealer or write for free catalog to Dept. GI, Dover Publications, Inc., 31 East 2nd St., Mineola, N.Y. 11501. Dover publishes more than 175 books each year on science, elementary and advanced mathematics, biology, music, art, literary history, social sciences and other areas.